This book
is in the care of:

Isaac Douglas
Woods

The STORYBOOK of GOD'S GREAT Love

Written by **LAURIN GRECO** ✳ Illustrated by **JEFF GREGORY**

FOREWORD BY CHARLES F. STANLEY

 In Touch Ministries

P.O. Box 7900
Atlanta, GA 30357
intouch.org

TABLE of CONTENTS

FOREWORD

The Bible tells us that after Joshua died, there was an entire generation "who knew neither the Lord nor what he had done for Israel" (Judges 2:10). Can you imagine that? Within the span of a few decades, parents no longer told their children the story of the Red Sea parting. There was no more reminiscing about heaven-sent manna and quail over breakfast. And on hot summer days, no one brought up the time God caused the sun to stand still in the sky. The Israelites didn't tell their children and grandchildren about the great deeds God had done for them—and as a result, those young people didn't know Him or His great love.

Friend, this book you hold in your hands is a spiritual weapon, and the enemy of God wants you to put it on a shelf somewhere in your home and forget about it. But my hope is that you will make this storybook a regular part of bedtime,

mealtime, or family devotions. My prayer is that it will spark meaningful conversations and bring your entire family closer to the Lord.

The stories on the pages that follow are taken from the Old Testament, retold and illustrated in a way that boys and girls can readily understand. They were selected to help young people take part in the unfolding story of redemption that God began writing in Genesis and continues to write in the lives of men, women, and children today. Above all, these stories were chosen to help a new generation come to know our heavenly Father and His love. God is good, and the child who learns to trust Him at a young age has discovered the path of life.

Charles F. Stanley

CHAPTER ONE

WHEN GOD SAID, "HELLO!"

God is good. | Genesis 1-2

Before there was anything—not our planet, not one bug, not even a speck of dirt—God was.

God has always been alive. Good and great and loving. God is so good that He wanted to make a whole universe that would show His goodness. So He did.

He sent planets spinning and whirling—so many that we haven't even seen them all yet! But God knows them, and He keeps each one moving–twirling and circling, part of a great, humongous dance.

God focused in on one empty planet: Earth! He was like a great painter standing before a blank canvas. He could make anything He wanted.

Then He spoke: "Light! Come to be!" And light did.

The light chased away the darkness. It was the very first day that ever was.

God spoke and made the sky and the ground and the seas.

"Next," He decided, "I want plants."

The ground burst with tall, tall trees and tiny blades of grass. Fireworks of color exploded—plants sprouted flowers and fruit! Peanuts and potatoes down in the dirt; eggplants and tomatoes up above the dirt. God's planet was alive and green.

Next, God made the sun, the moon, and the stars.

"This sun will pour out light and warmth over the day," He decided. "This moon will stand guard at night."

Then He sent forth millions of massive stars—no, billions! And God knows them all by name.

Then God turned His attention back to our planet. "The seas need swimmers, and the skies need flyers," He proclaimed. And all of a sudden, they were.

The seas brimmed with life—whales sang, seahorses bobbed, penguins splashed, clams clammed, and crabs scuttled.

The skies flitted with birds, and the planet filled with song as canaries and cardinals and chickadees tweeted their tunes.

"Now it's time to fill the land," God decided. Suddenly, horses galloped across the countryside. Giraffes stretched tall for leaves. Elephants sprayed water with their fun new trunks. Turtles took their time on their walks. Kangaroos tested their jumping legs. The earth was filled with play.

It was wonderful, it was beautiful, but God wasn't finished. "It's time for something really special," God declared. "This final creation of Mine will be different, set apart. I want them to think and talk and love, just like Me. They'll be My friends."

So He took some dirt and shaped it. Then He put His face down near the earth and blew His very own breath into the dirt He had shaped.

A man! And then, a little while later, a woman!

They loved and talked and laughed, God's close friends.

Creation—God's beautiful invention—was finished. And God rested.

God's masterpiece has a message, and if you look and listen closely, you can hear it: "God is good!" is woven within the bird's song. "God is good!" is displayed in the lion's strength. "God is good!" echoes in the puppy's yip. "God is good!" shines through the bright red rose. All these things are good because God is good.

And that is the secret in God's great "Hello!" When God first introduced Himself, when He first showed who He is, He showed that He is good. Out of His good heart overflowed goodness.

This is the most important truth you can ever remember. It's the most important thing God wants you to know: He is very, very, very good.

CHAPTER TWO

THE DAY EVERYTHING BROKE

We have an enemy who wants us to doubt God's heart.
Genesis 3

*G*od and His friends, *Adam and Eve,* were happy and close.

God had made a garden filled with trees that grew the juiciest, tastiest fruits. It was Adam and Eve's home. In the middle of the

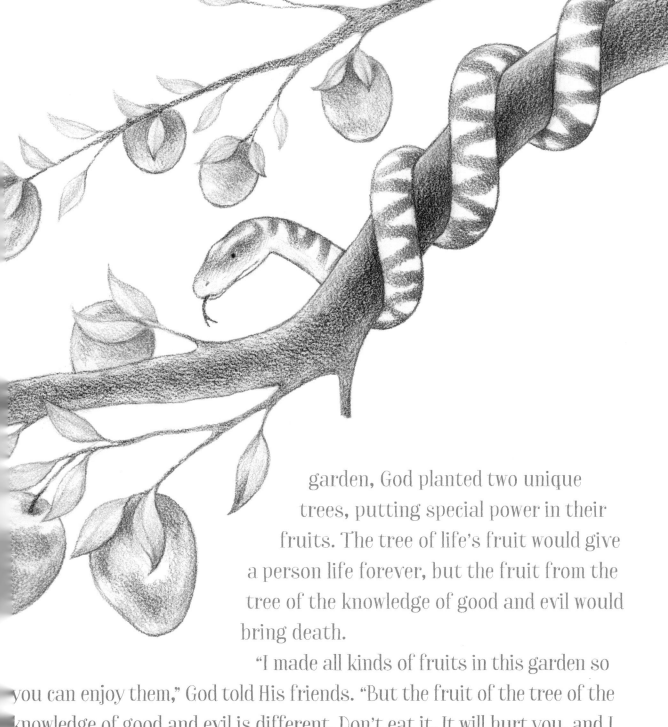

garden, God planted two unique trees, putting special power in their fruits. The tree of life's fruit would give a person life forever, but the fruit from the tree of the knowledge of good and evil would bring death.

"I made all kinds of fruits in this garden so you can enjoy them," God told His friends. "But the fruit of the tree of the knowledge of good and evil is different. Don't eat it. It will hurt you, and I don't want you to get hurt."

There was one being who couldn't stand all of the happiness God had made: Satan. While God loves joy and goodness, Satan delights in hurt and pain. He hates God and wants to hurt God and His friends.

As a snake, he slithered into God's garden, right up to Eve. "What's this God says about not being able to eat fruit in the garden?" he asked.

"That's not what God said," Eve answered. "We can eat any fruit we want—just not fruit from this one tree. It will hurt us."

"But the fruit of this tree won't hurt you. It will help you know what's good and what isn't," the serpent lied. It was as if he were aiming a poison arrow straight at Eve's heart. The serpent continued, "That sounds to me like a good thing. God must be keeping something good from you."

God must be keeping something good from you. That's because He isn't really good. That poison lie seeped deep into Eve's heart. And it started to work. She wondered, *Maybe God is keeping something good from me. If He was good, He would want me to have every good thing. Is He good? He must not be.*

Eve doubted God's good heart. So she picked a fruit from the tree God said not to eat from and took a bite. Adam was with her, and he took a bite, too.

It was the first sin.

Right that very instant, something in Adam and Eve broke. They could feel it. They had only ever been happy, but an awful feeling sank into their stomachs. They felt unbeautiful, unloved, and ashamed. The saddest thing of all is what they felt but couldn't name: Their sin had broken their closeness with God.

God had warned them that eating the fruit would hurt them, and it did. Deeply.

Adam and Eve broke.

The world broke.

And God's heart broke, too.

Adam and Eve ran and hid, too ashamed to stay in the open of God's wonderful garden. Even though they had hurt Him, God came looking for His friends. He didn't want them to be scared or ashamed.

God spoke to the evil serpent. "Serpent, you are always going to be the enemy of people. But one day a Person is going to come. While you will hurt Him, He will crush you, once and for all." God was going to rescue His people from Satan and his lies—forever.

Then God spoke to His broken friends: "You can't stay here in the garden, because if you eat the fruit of the tree of life, you'll live forever. And I don't want you to be broken forever."

So God, sad and heavy-hearted, made His friends leave their beautiful garden home for their own good. It was a sad, sad day.

God isn't really good. It's the poison lie that breaks everything. We hear it a lot in our hearts. Like Adam and Eve, we have an enemy who tries to make us believe it. He wants us to doubt God's good heart. But it's an awful lie.

Don't ever listen to the poison lie. No matter how you feel or what you think, this is what is always, always true: God is good. He is the best good that anyone could be. And He loves you very much.

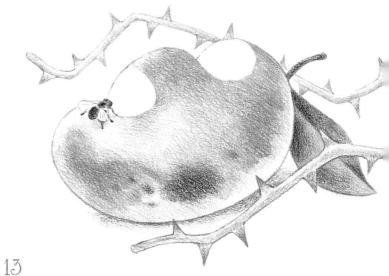

13

CHAPTER THREE

THE RAINIEST DAYS

God is good, so He hates anything evil.
Genesis 6:9-9:19

*A*dam and Eve's children—and their children's children—didn't realize it, but they were very, very sick. They were sick with sin. Their closeness with God was broken. Something inside of them always told them to do evil.

Instead of being kind to people, they were mean. Instead of telling the truth, something told them to lie. The whole world soon became filled with bullies and liars and thieves. Everyone had an ugly heart.

And it made God very sad. He had created each person with tender care, and His heart ached as He watched them hurt each other. "I am sorry I ever made people," He said.

But God's heart lifted when He thought about the one person on earth who loved Him: Noah.

Noah loved God and God's goodness. So like God, Noah was honest and noble, kind and giving.

"Noah," God said to His friend, "everyone else in the world has a heart that wants to do evil—all the time. They can't be rescued, and they aren't going to change. So I'm going to bring a giant flood to wash the whole earth clean. But, I promise, I will save you and your family. Once all of the evil is washed away, we're going to start over.

"So build an ark. There needs to be enough room for your family, plus two of every creature. And food, too."

Hmm, Noah thought. *I've never built an ark. I'm not sure how I'm going to gather all of those animals. Or get all of their food. But I love God, and I know that He is good.*

"I will do everything You say, God," Noah answered.

Faithfully, Noah started planning and measuring and chopping and building. *Chop, chop, chop. Chisel, chisel, chisel. Pound, pound, pound.* Noah, his three sons, and their wives worked and worked, doing their best to get everything ready, just as God had said.

Even though Noah didn't know how to build an ark, God guided him. Plank by plank, deck by deck. And even though Noah didn't know how he was going to gather all the animals, God brought them to him— from aardvarks and ants to zebras and zebus. And even though Noah didn't know where he was going to get the food for all those creatures, God provided it. Noah trusted God with what he didn't know. And God took care of His friend.

"Noah, it's time to get in the ark," God said. So Noah, his family, and all of the creatures climbed inside. God Himself shut the door.

It rained. And it rained. Really, really hard–for 40 days and 40 nights. The waters rose higher and higher, washing away everything but the ark. God protected it. It floated safely on top of the waves.

After 150 days, the ark came to rest on a mountain. "Noah, bring everything out of the ark," God told His friend. It was the most unique celebration of squawking and squealing and strutting and soaring you've ever seen. The elephants stretched their legs and the flamingoes tested their wings. Noah's family breathed in the fresh, clean air.

"Noah, I want every couple to start a family," God said. "I made this planet to be enjoyed. Fill the earth with people and animals once again." The fresh start was beginning.

God told Noah, "I am good and fair. I can't let evil walk all over goodness. Evil must be punished. And sadly, there will be evil again. But I am making you a promise. I will never again destroy the world with a flood. I am giving you the rainbow as a sign of my promise. Every time you see it in the sky, you can know that no matter how hard it rains, it's going to stop."

Every time there's a rainbow in the sky, God remembers His promise. And every time there's a rainbow, you can remember God's promise, too.

There's something very special about a rainbow. It looks just like a drawn bow–like a bow from a bow and arrow, pointing toward heaven. God knew that people would do more evil; they would sin again. But this time, God Himself would take the punishment, the arrow. And He did. On the cross, Jesus took the arrow for you, paying for all your sins. Because He loves you very much.

CHAPTER FOUR

THE TROUBLE BETWEEN TWINS

God wants you to forgive other people,
even when they've hurt you deeply.

Genesis 27, 32-33

Jacob had done an awful, awful thing. His twin brother, Esau, was set to be the head of the family when their father died because he was the oldest son. He would get most of the family's wealth.

Jacob knew this. And one day when Esau was out hunting, he carried out a sneaky plan. He dressed up like his brother and convinced his blind father, Isaac, that he was his twin. Isaac fell for it.

Isaac spoke the family blessing over Jacob when it was supposed to be for Esau. Now Jacob would get most of the family wealth.

This made Esau hopping mad. Hopping, hopping, hopping mad. Jacob had just stolen his future.

Jacob couldn't stay at home—his brother was out to get him! So Jacob ran away. And he stayed away—for 20 long years. While he was away, he started a huge family and raised herds of cows, donkeys, sheep, and goats. Until one day ...

"Jacob," God said. "It's time for you to go home. Go back to your family and your family's land. I will be with you."

Jacob was nervous. And afraid. But he obeyed God. He packed up his family—he had 11 sons and a daughter!—and all of their tents and belongings. He gathered all of his animals ... hundreds of cows, donkeys, sheep, and goats! They formed a huge caravan as they started the long journey back home.

The closer Jacob got to his home, the more nervous he got. *Esau must hate me,* he thought. When Jacob's caravan was approaching Esau, Jacob sent out servants with a kind message. Maybe it would smooth out the rough waters.

But the messengers returned back with disturbing news. "Your brother Esau is close. He is coming this way—and he has 400 men with him!"

Four hundred men! Jacob's heart sank. *That's an army!* Esau could wipe out Jacob's entire family if he wanted to.

Jacob thought up a plan as quickly as he could. *Maybe a huge gift would make things better!* He had his herdsmen count out over 200 goats, 200 sheep, 30 camels, 50 cows, and 20 donkeys. Jacob sent them ahead of the clan to Esau.

Jacob's caravan kept on trudging closer and closer to Esau. Soon Jacob was able to see Esau and his 400 men looming powerfully on the horizon. And before long, Jacob was close enough to see his brother's face. But Jacob couldn't read Esau's emotions. Was he still angry? Would his army hurt Jacob's family? Jacob bowed low before Esau seven times, honoring him.

Esau took off, sprinting toward his brother. Jacob stood up, bracing himself for what was coming. Esau threw his arms around Jacob. He wasn't attacking him—it was a big bear hug! Esau was happy! Tears streamed down their faces as they sobbed. "All is well, brother," Esau choked out. "I have forgiven you."

Esau tried to return Jacob's huge gift. He wanted Jacob to know that he had forgiven him completely. But Jacob would have nothing of it. He was so grateful for his brother's forgiveness.

God knew that Esau needed to forgive and that Jacob needed to know he was forgiven. And even though Jacob had stolen something precious from his brother, their relationship was healed, because Esau didn't make Jacob pay for the great debt he owed him. Esau's relationship with his brother was more important than all the riches of the family blessing.

There will be people in this broken world who will hurt you deeply. And when that happens, it's okay to be sad over what was taken from you. What you lose matters. When you hurt, it's a reminder that the good world God created is broken.

It's important to God that you forgive that person for what they took from you. He doesn't want your heart stuck in anger or hurt. Forgiveness is a way of shaking the chains off your heart, and God wants your heart to be free!

Forgiveness reverses evil. It gives goodness for something bad. That's what God does with us.

God is a Master at forgiving. So ask Him for help when you need to forgive. And ask Him to heal your hurting heart, too. Those are prayers He really wants to answer because He loves you so much and wants you to be free.

CHAPTER FIVE

THE STORY OF THE GOOD IN THE BAD

God uses all hard things for good.
Genesis 37, 39-47, 50

Joseph had 11 brothers, but his father, Jacob, loved Joseph most of all. Jacob even gave him an ornate coat so everyone could see Joseph was his dad's favorite. His brothers were jealous.

"We've got to get that Joseph," the brothers schemed. One day, while they were out in the fields shepherding, they ripped Joseph's beautiful coat off him and shoved him down, down, down into a dark and empty well. Soon, a caravan of traders came by. "This man is for sale," the brothers told them.

Joseph never saw his home again.

Life was very hard as a slave. But it got even harder when Joseph was accused of a crime he didn't commit. Even though he had done nothing wrong, Joseph was thrown down, down, down into a dark and

lonely dungeon.

Had God abandoned Joseph? It might seem that way. But even though Joseph couldn't see Him, God was right there with him. Out of horrible, hard things, God was making something very good.

God made it so the man who ran the prison liked Joseph very much. "I'm putting you in charge of all the prisoners," the jailer told him.

After Joseph had been in prison for years and years, the wine taster and baker to the king of Egypt were thrown into the very same jail. One night, the men had strange dreams. God told Joseph what they meant. And three days later, both men were released from jail, just as Joseph said.

The wine taster had promised not to forget Joseph. But he forgot. And Joseph stayed in jail for two … more … long … years.

But then Pharaoh, the king of Egypt, had a strange dream, too. "I know someone who can tell you what your dream means," the royal wine taster told Pharaoh. Soon Joseph found himself lifted up out of the dark, dank prison and standing before the most powerful man in the world.

Once again, God was with Joseph. He told him the meaning of Pharaoh's dream. In the dream there were lots of cows. "Those seven healthy, plump cows that you dreamed about?" Joseph explained. "There will be seven

years with plenty of food. And those seven skinny, sickly cows? Afterwards, there will be seven years without any food."

Pharaoh was impressed with Joseph. "I'm putting you in charge of all Egypt," the Pharaoh said. Joseph was second only to Pharaoh himself! Pharaoh even dressed Joseph in fine robes—like the beautiful coat his dad had given him years before.

Joseph got the nation ready for the famine by storing up grain during the years when there was plenty. And when the famine came, Egypt was the only place that had food.

Back home, Joseph's brothers were hungry. So they came to Egypt—and stood before Joseph—to ask for something to eat. They bowed before their brother, though they didn't recognize him. But Joseph knew exactly who they were.

He cleared all of the royal servants out of the room. Then he wept so hard his sobs echoed down the halls. "I'm your long lost brother!" he cried. "I'm Joseph!"

The brothers were stunned. *This is Joseph?* They were worried. Surely he would punish them for what they had done.

"No! Don't worry, brothers," Joseph said. "I'm not going to punish you. You did something very evil, yes. But now I see. God is so good that He used even your evil to do something wonderful. Now bring our entire family to Egypt—please bring Dad, too. God has provided food, and we will ride out this famine together. As a family."

This family was a very special family. It was the family that Moses would come from. And Joshua, Gideon, and Hannah. David, Elisha, and Hezekiah, too! Most of the people we read about in the Bible were from Joseph's family—even God's own Son, Jesus! God used the hard things Joseph went through to save that family—the family of the One who would save us all.

In everything that happens in your life—including the hard and the unfair things—God is working for good. Since God is so good, it's impossible for Him to do anything but good. So when things get difficult, do everything you can to remind your heart that He is using every hard thing to do something wonderful.

God will be so happy that you trusted Him. And then, once it's all over, like Joseph, you'll be able to see the good that God has been working on all along.

CHAPTER SIX

GOD MAKES A WAY

God wants you to know He is more powerful than anything.
Exodus 12:31-15:21

After a long life, Joseph died and went home to God. But his family lived in Egypt for hundreds of years. They kept having babies and grew into an entire nation!

The Egyptians became afraid that Joseph's huge family was going to take over Egypt. So they made them slaves. "Help us, God!" Joseph's family cried. God answered because He loved His special family.

God chose a shepherd named Moses to lead the people out of slavery. Moses listened to God and spoke His words. "God wants you to let His people go," Moses told Pharaoh, the king of Egypt. But Pharaoh was stubborn. He wouldn't listen.

God showed how
serious He was 10 times,
doing 10 powerful things so
Pharaoh could see that He is the
true King. God even caused it to rain
frogs! Soon, Pharaoh wanted nothing
more than to have God's people leave.
"Get out! Get out right now!" Pharaoh
ordered. God's people packed up in a hurry.
God was setting them free!
God had a special home prepared for His
people. Since they had to travel through the desert
to get there, God put a tall, skinny cloud in front of them
that touched the ground and stretched up to the sky. It moved and
led the way. At night, the tall cloud turned into a glowing, fiery pillar–a
massive night light. All of the grandpas, grandmas, daddies, mommies,
kids, and babies of God's special family, along with their animals, followed

along in a huge caravan. It was the world's biggest camping trip.

After a few days of traveling, God told Moses to do something strange. "I want you to turn back and camp on the shore of the Red Sea." It was an odd request. Why should they go backwards? But God's pillar led the people to the edge of the sea.

Meanwhile, back in Egypt, Pharaoh was questioning his decision to let God's people go. "What was I thinking? We need our slaves to get work done! I'm going to bring them back to Egypt where they belong!"

In a flash, all of his chariots, horsemen, and soldiers got ready. "Let's get our slaves!" Pharoah commanded. And they barreled through the desert after God's people.

But God's people weren't moving. God was directing them to be still, to camp on the bank of the sea.

Rumble, rumble, rumble. God's people felt the ground shaking. Soon, they could see the horses and chariots on the horizon, led by Pharaoh himself. The Egyptians were coming after them! They were getting closer and closer! And God's people had nowhere to go—they were trapped with their backs to the Red Sea!

Panic spread through the camp. "We should have never left Egypt!" God's people cried to Moses. "We're going to die!"

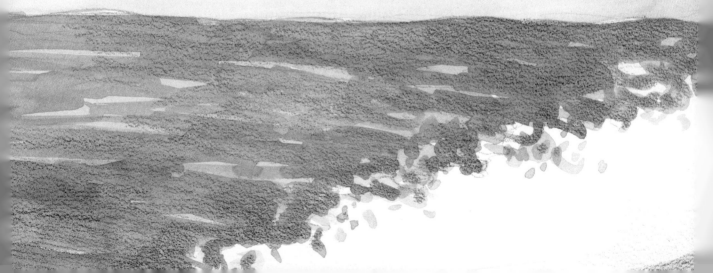

"Don't forget God!" Moses answered. "He loves you, and He is going to fight for you. Just be still and watch Him do something amazing!"

"Raise your staff above the water, Moses," God said.

Suddenly the wind whipped up all around the people. *Whoosh!* It blew their clothes, their hair. And it also blew the sea, pushing it back, back, back until there was a path through the water. God was making a way for His people to escape!

"Let's go!" And the entire caravan of people and animals began to walk through the walls of water on dry land.

"After them!" Pharaoh shouted. And the Egyptian army thundered after God's people down the path through the sea.

God's people arrived safely on the other side. "Moses, reach out your hand over the sea," God told him. And *whoosh!* God released the waters. The Egyptian army was washed away for good.

As the sun rose, God's people danced and sang for joy.

God can do anything. God put His people in a situation that seemed impossible—and He did it on purpose. He wanted them to see that there is nothing He can't do. God wants you to know the same thing, too. So if you're facing something tough and there seems to be no way out, trust Him, trust Him, trust Him. He loves to make a way when there isn't one.

CHAPTER SEVEN

GOD'S GOOD FRIEND

God wants you to know who He is.
Exodus 16-17, 33-34

God's people, safe from the Egyptians, followed God's pillar of cloud and fire through the wilderness. They were headed to their new home! But their journey took them through the desert, where very little food grows.

"We're hungry," God's people said. And God heard them.

Six mornings a week, God put honey bread on the ground for breakfast. God's people would come out of their tents in the morning, stretching and wiping the sleep from their eyes. And the honey bread flakes would be right there on the ground—special delivery breakfast! Five days a week, everyone gathered just enough bread for that day. And on the sixth day, they'd

gather twice as much so they could rest on the seventh day.

And every evening, God sent flocks of quail for dinner. *Flutter, flutter, flutter.* Special delivery dinner! Every night, God's people would sit around their campfires eating their tender quail.

And for water, God directed Moses to strike a rock. *Gush!* Water poured out. Families came to fill up their water skins, and the flocks and herds would sip from the pools that had collected. God's people were seeing His goodness. He took care of their every single need, every single day.

Moses, the people's leader, was learning about God, too. Outside of the camp, he set up a tent. He and God met inside. They talked for hours because they were good, good friends.

"God," Moses said one day, "I want to know more about You. Please tell me more about who You are. Will You show me?"

"I will," God answered. "I will let all of My goodness pass before you. But I can't let you see My face. It's so powerfully perfect that it would overwhelm you. So tomorrow, go up to the top of Mount Sinai. There is a place there where you can hide in the rock. I will pass by you and tell you who I am. To protect you, I will cover you with My hand."

Moses did just as God had said. Early the next morning, he left all of the people behind, sleeping in their tents. He climbed and climbed up to the very top of Mount Sinai. And there was the cleft in the rock, just like God had said. He tucked himself inside the space—solid rock on the right, solid rock on the left. Then, he waited.

Suddenly a thick, thick cloud enveloped Moses, fogging everything he could see. The ground underneath him shook. The rocks surrounding him shook. A powerful wave of love washed over Moses. God was passing by.

God called out: "I am God. My name is Yahweh. I am good and kind. I do not get angry quickly. I am full of love, so very full of love. I have so much love that I spill it out onto people, and I forgive anyone who asks. But since I love what's good, I don't let evil go unpunished."

Overwhelmed with awe and joy, Moses dropped to his knees. "God, You are so wonderful! I want to follow You all of my life. So do these people I'm leading. There is no one as good and as loving as You are."

God is the King of everything. But when Moses, one of the countless people He had made, asked to know more about Him, God responded. He answered Moses' request, even though He didn't have to. That's because God loved Moses.

God loves you, too, and He wants you to know who He is. That's one of the big reasons He gave us the Bible. Even though He is the most powerful Being who exists, He doesn't want to be a mystery. He wants you to know what His heart is like—what brings Him joy, what makes Him sad, and what makes Him laugh.

God likes you so much and wants to be your good Friend. He wants to spend time with you, to talk to you about everything. There is nothing better than being God's friend because God is the best Friend of all.

CHAPTER EIGHT

THE GIRL WHO MADE GOD HAPPY

God wants everyone to be a part of His family.

Joshua 2

God led His special family to the land He had promised to give them—the Promised Land! But there were powerful and wicked people already living there.

God's people got scared. "We can't go in there! Those people are too strong!"

After all God's people had seen Him do, they still didn't trust Him fully. It broke God's heart. So to help His special family learn how to trust Him, they wandered in the desert for 40 long years.

Sand, sand, and more sand. Forty years of sand. During those 40 years, God took care of His people. And a new generation grew up. Maybe this generation would trust Him.

Joshua, the people's new leader, sent two spies into the mighty city of Jericho to learn about it. It would need to be conquered for God's people to settle into the Promised Land.

The spies scouted out the city. "We need a safe place to stay for the night," one said to the other as darkness closed in.

"Come with me," they heard a woman whisper.

The woman's name was Rahab, and she was putting herself in grave danger helping the spies. But she allowed them to stay in her home with her family.

Pound, pound, pound. Rahab's door shook as men sent from the king demanded to be let in.

"Quickly!" Rahab said, leading the two spies up onto the roof. "Hide under these piles of straw! I will do my best to protect you!"

Rahab scurried downstairs and opened the door for the king's men. "Where are the spies?" they demanded. But Rahab didn't tell them where they were. The king's soldiers ran off to continue their hunt, and Rahab climbed back upstairs onto the roof.

"I know you're spies," she said to the two men, as they dusted themselves off. "And I also know you're members of God's family. I've heard of the great things God has done for your people—like how He parted the Red Sea to rescue you. And I know He is very powerful. I believe He is going to hand this city over to you. Please, let me make one request. When God gives you this city, remember me and my family."

"We will," the spies promised. "Keep what we're doing a secret. When you hear our armies attacking, bring your family inside of this home. Then place a scarlet cord out the window. When our armies see the red cord, they'll know not to bring harm to your family. Since you've protected us, we'll protect you."

God's people had seen Him do incredible miracles with their very eyes, but Rahab wasn't a part of God's special family. She had only heard about the things God had done. But she believed in God anyway. And it made God very happy.

God protected Rahab. He was so impressed with her that He brought her into His special family. In fact, He placed Rahab into a very important family tree—the family tree of His one and only Son. God made Rahab Jesus' great-great-many-times-great grandmother.

Like Rahab,
God wants
everyone
to believe in
Him and be
a part of His
family. Every
single person
you know, and
even people who
live far, far away,
whom you don't
know—God loves, loves,
loves them. Think of some
people who aren't a part of
God's family. Ask God to help them
believe in Him, like Rahab did, so they
can become a part of His special family.
It's the very best family, and it lasts
forever and ever!

CHAPTER NINE

THE DAY GOD GAVE STRANGE COMMANDS

Obey God, even when you don't understand.

Joshua 6

Joshua looked up, and up and up. The walls around the city of Jericho were so tall! And strong! God's people wanted to settle into their new home, but they had to get past Jericho. The city stood like a mighty soldier, arms crossed, guarding the land.

The high, thick walls weren't letting anyone pass. The gates were locked up tight. How would God's people ever conquer this city?

It looked impossible.

But it wasn't impossible for God.

Cities rise and cities fall because God is in charge of them all. God could have given Joshua the city of Jericho in a heartbeat. He could have just thought it, and it would have happened! But He wanted His people to trust in Him—no matter what.

"Joshua," God told His people's leader, "I have a special battle plan that I want you to follow." God told Joshua, step by step, exactly what to do. They were very odd plans for a battle against a mighty city. Joshua didn't understand, but he trusted God anyway.

The sun was rising the next morning as Joshua prepared the army. "Rise and shine! Get ready! Today we go to battle against Jericho!" he proclaimed. The men strapped on their weapons, ready for battle. "Charge the walls!" they were expecting to hear. But Joshua's next orders—God's special instructions—surprised everyone. "March around the city ... without talking!"

Huh? God's people didn't understand. At all. But they got in their battle lines and prepared to march.

"Forward march!" Joshua ordered. *Left, right, left, right, left, right, left* went the footsteps on the ground as the army marched around the city, not speaking one word. "Blow the trumpets!" Joshua commanded the priests, just like God had instructed. The blasts of the trumpets pierced the air, echoing for miles around. It was a declaration. God's people were on the move.

The army walked around the walls one time, ready for Joshua's next command. But Joshua stopped the march. He didn't issue an order to charge the walls. Instead, he ordered everyone back into camp. "What are God's people doing?" the people of Jericho wondered aloud.

The next morning at sunrise: "Rise and shine!" God's people got up and did the same thing. "Forward march!" And they did the same thing the next day, and the next day, and the next day, and the next day. It was the oddest battle strategy anyone had ever seen.

On the seventh day, the sun rose. "Rise and shine!" And the army began to march again. "Forward march!" *Left, right, left, right, left, right, left.* "Blow the trumpets!" Joshua commanded. The air filled with the blasts. The army finished their lap around the walls. But this time Joshua didn't stop the march. "March around the city again!" he ordered. So the army kept marching. They marched around the city again. And again. And again. And again. And again.

When the army began to march around

the city the seventh time, Joshua gave a signal. The priests blew their trumpets as long and loud as they could. "Everyone shout!" Joshua ordered.

And boy, did they! God's people shouted the loudest, rumbliest roar you've ever heard.

The ground shook. The knees of the people of Jericho shook. And the strong, tall walls shook.

Rumble, rumble, rumble. The walls started to crack. Then they started to crumble. Then they started to fall.

All of the sudden, the tall, powerful walls that once seemed impossible to Joshua's army crumbled into piles at their feet. When the dust settled, God's people and the people of Jericho found themselves staring at each other. And one thing became clear to everyone: Nothing is impossible for the mighty, powerful, and awesome God.

Always, always, always follow God's instructions. They may seem strange. They may not make any sense to you or to other people. (Who attacks a city by taking a walk?) But God knows much more than what you know–He knows *everything!* He sees much more than what you can see–He sees *everything!* He can do much more than what you can do– He can do *anything!* And He's always up to something good. So His ways are always, always, always best.

Trust God's knowledge. Trust God's sight. Trust God's power. And trust God's good heart. When you obey Him no matter what, you'll find out, as God's people did, that He will take care of everything. And He will lead you on the best, wildest, and most beautiful adventure of all.

CHAPTER TEN

THE MIGHTY WARRIOR WHO WAS SCARED

God wants to help you trust Him when you're afraid.

Judges 6

Afraid, *Gideon looked* to his left and to his right. *Is anyone watching?* he wondered. Gideon was preparing what little wheat his family had left, and he didn't want any of his wicked neighbors to steal it.

You see, there were evil people living in the Promised Land. God's special family was supposed to drive them out. But they didn't. They let some stay.

So God's people had awful neighbors. "Don't follow God. Follow our gods," these neighbors said. But their gods were really no gods at all. They only wanted to lead people far away from the one and only true God.

These bad neighbors rubbed off on God's people. It was terrible. And God was so sad. God's people were showing that they didn't want Him.

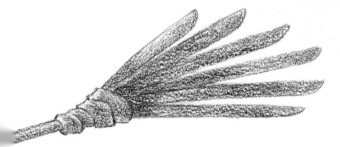

So God honored their choice.

He let their evil neighbors do what evil neighbors do: attack and steal. And God didn't step in.

One group of neighbors, the Midianites, kept attacking. And attacking. They destroyed all of the crops. They stole all of the livestock. They took almost everything. "Help us, God!" His people cried. And God heard them.

God had a plan, and that plan involved a hero who didn't think he was a hero: a young man named Gideon.

Gideon was hiding, preparing his family's wheat out of the sight of the evil Midianites, when suddenly, an angel appeared. "Mighty warrior!" the angel boomed. Gideon looked around. Surely the angel was talking about someone else. "Mighty warrior! God is with you! And you're going to rescue God's people from these evil enemies."

"With all due respect, sir," Gideon replied, "I think you have the wrong person. I'm not a warrior at all. I'm not strong or brave. I'm hiding!"

"Don't be afraid," the angel answered. "God is with you. And He is going to be with you when you fight the Midianites."

Gideon tried his best to believe the angel, but he was still scared. A little while later, he heard that enemy neighbors were joining together to attack God's people. "This must be when God wants me to lead," he gulped.

"God," Gideon prayed, "You said that You wanted me to lead Your people to defeat our enemies. But I'm so scared. Are You sure You want *me?*

"Will You do something for me that will help my scared heart? See, I have this wool fleece here. I'm going to leave it outside overnight. When I wake up, if the fleece is wet and the ground is dry, that's how I'll know that You really are choosing me."

Gideon put out his fleece and went to sleep.

God heard Gideon's prayer, and He saw His friend was scared. God wanted Gideon to know He was with him, even though Gideon couldn't see Him.

When Gideon woke up, he picked up his fleece, first thing. *Drip, drip drip.* It was as wet as if he'd just pulled it out of a bucket of water. But the ground was bone dry. God had done exactly what he had asked!

"God, thank You for answering me," Gideon prayed, "but, You see,

I'm still scared. Really scared. So would You mind doing one more thing? This time, when I put the fleece out, will You make it completely dry while the ground is soaking wet? Then I'll know for sure that You want me."

Once again, Gideon put out his fleece that night and went to sleep.

Squish, squish, squish went the ground as Gideon walked up to his fleece first thing the next morning. But his fleece was so dry he could have used it as a towel. God had answered—again!

"Okay, God," Gideon said. "I'm still scared, but I know You're with me. And I'll do everything You ask."

Gideon trusted God. He gathered up an army and led God's people to fight—and God set His people free from the Midianites.

Like Gideon, when you're scared, you can always talk to God. God wants you to come to Him. He isn't mad at you because you're nervous or afraid. He wants to help you know that He is with you.

So when you're scared, talk to God about what you're afraid of. Be honest, even if it's hard. And ask Him for help. You might be weak, but that's okay. In God's power, you too are a mighty warrior.

CHAPTER ELEVEN

The Girl Who Moved God's Heart

God loves it when you share your heart with Him.

1 Samuel 1:1-2:26

Even after Gideon's victory, bad neighbors kept pulling God's people further and further away from Him. Soon, hardly anyone loved God at all.

This went on for years and years. God was so sad. It hurts terribly to love someone when they don't love you back.

But there was a woman who loved God very much. Her name was Hannah. And her love was a bright spot in all of the darkness.

Hannah loved God, she loved her husband, and her husband loved her. But even with all of this love, Hannah was very sad. You see, Hannah wanted a baby. But after being married for years, she didn't have one, even though a child was what she wanted more than anything in all the world.

Every year, Hannah and her husband would travel to the special town where God's people went to worship Him. One year, on one of those trips, a mean woman made fun of Hannah for not having any children. Hannah was crushed. Hurt. Devastated. Tears streaming down her face, she went to God's house to be with Him.

Once there, Hannah couldn't keep her feelings bottled up. She wept and sobbed as she poured out her heart to God, her Friend.

"God, I want a baby so badly. And I know that You are the King of

everything. Please give me a child. And if You do, I promise that I will give Him back to You. He will serve You as long as he lives. I promise."

The head priest who was in charge of God's house, Eli, watched Hannah as she cried and prayed. He could tell that something was troubling her. "Young woman," he said, "may God give you what you have asked Him for."

Hannah's family soon headed back home, and in the course of time, God gave Hannah a baby—a baby boy. God had heard her! And she wanted the world to know. So she named him Samuel, which means, "heard by God."

As Samuel grew, Hannah taught him about God's goodness. "God is good, and He loves you very much," she sang to him as she rocked him. "God gave us this food because He loves us," she told him before every meal. "God is watering our crops," she explained each time it rained. Little Samuel grew up understanding God's good heart because Hannah taught him about it, just like she promised she would.

When Samuel was old enough to live apart from his mother and father, Hannah's family took their yearly visit to God's house. Eli the priest was there, just as he had been years before.

"I am the woman who was crying and crying here those many years ago," Hannah told him. "God heard my prayer and answered me. He gave me this son, Samuel. I raised Samuel to love and follow God, just as I promised I would. Samuel loves God very much, and he is here to stay with you at God's house where he will help other people worship."

Samuel stayed at God's house with Eli. And every year when Hannah came to visit and worship God, she gave Samuel a new garment she had made for him.

Samuel grew up to be one of the greatest of God's prophets who ever lived. (A prophet is a person who hears from God and speaks His messages.) Samuel helped turn many of God's people back to Him.

God gave Samuel to Hannah, and Hannah gave him back to God. God was so moved by Hannah's goodness that He blessed her even more. He gave her not one, not two, but *five* more babies. God made sure her heart was full, as well as her home.

God loves when you come to Him and share everything that is on your heart. And He loves to answer your prayers with good things. While He may not answer you exactly the way you expect, He will always give you what He knows is best. God loves you, and when you love Him back—like Hannah did—you'll find that He will fill your heart and your life with the very best things.

CHAPTER TWELVE

THE SHEPHERD WHOM GOD CHOSE TO BE KING

God cares about what's in your heart.
1 Samuel 16-17

"*Samuel,*" *God told the prophet,* "I'm going to show you who is to be the next king. He is one of Jesse's sons."

"Yes, God," Samuel answered. And he went to Bethlehem, the town where Jesse lived. Soon, he was looking up, up, up at a tall, strapping young man—Jesse's oldest son.

Surely this is the one God wants to be king, Samuel thought. *What a perfect choice.* "No, Samuel," God answered him in his heart. "This isn't My choice for the next king. I know he looks very kingly. But the way a person looks on the outside isn't what is most important to Me. What

matters most to Me is on the inside, in their heart."

So Samuel called for Jesse's next son. Then the next. Then the next. All seven of Jesse's sons walked before Samuel, but God didn't pick any of them.

"Do you have any more sons?" Samuel asked, turning to Jesse.

"Well, there is the youngest. He's out watching the sheep," Jesse answered.

"Bring him here please," Samuel replied.

A little while later, young David arrived. He was breathless from running and smelled like sheep.

"This is him," Samuel heard God's familiar voice in his heart.

"Yes, Lord," Samuel answered. He took the special oil used for declaring kings and poured it over the top of David's head. It ran through his hair, down his face, over his clothes. It dripped everywhere. Everyone around knew what it meant. David would be the next king of God's people.

But David didn't become king for a long, long time. Even so, he tucked what had happened into his heart, and he trusted God.

One day, enemies of God's people—the Philistines—came to do battle. The Philistine army stood on one hill. The king of God's people, King Saul, lined up his army on another. A valley stood between them. The men glowered at each other.

David's three oldest brothers were a part of the army. David, as the youngest, stayed at home to look after the sheep. But one day, his dad sent him to the front lines to bring his brothers some food. David arrived just as the armies were lining up for battle.

"Why do you even bother trying to fight the mighty Philistines?" David heard from the valley below. A giant of a man, more than nine feet tall, stood in bronze armor, spear in his hand, thundering at the top of his lungs.

"That's Goliath," one of the men next to David explained. "He's the strongest warrior of all the Philistines. He has yelled this same message every day for 40 days. We are all afraid of him."

"Come out and fight me, if you dare," Goliath roared. "If just one of your men can defeat me, all of us Philistines will serve you."

He's mocking God's people, David thought. *That means he's making fun of God! And God is way more powerful than that measly man—no matter how big his muscles are. I've got to do something about this!*

David went to King Saul. "Don't worry about that noisy Philistine," David told him. "God can defeat him in a heartbeat! I will go fight him!"

"You can't fight him," Saul replied. "You're just a boy."

"This man is mocking God—the mighty and powerful God," David responded. "God will triumph over him! I know it! Let me fight."

King Saul offered David his armor, but David turned it down. He picked up five smooth rocks and his slingshot, and sprinted down the hill to face the giant.

"Why do you send a puny boy to fight me?" Goliath laughed—a bellowing evil laugh. "I'm going to crush you into bird food."

Before Goliath could say another word, David put a rock in his sling and flung it. It hit Goliath squarely between the eyes, and the mighty giant fell flat on his face like a felled tree. *Thud!* The giant was dead. God's army had won.

David wasn't strong, but God is—and David knew it. So he stood up to Goliath, trusting that God would show His strength and power. And God loved it. In the Bible, David is the one and only person whom God calls a man after His very own heart.

Do you want to make God smile? Trust in Him. Know He is good. Know He is powerful. And believe in His goodness and power, no matter what. And you'll be a kid after God's own heart, too.

CHAPTER THIRTEEN

THE COMMANDER & THE GIRL WHO GREW LOVE

God wants you to show other people His love.

2 Kings 5:1-19

Once there was a girl who loved her life. She loved her family—even her family's stubborn ox. Home was her favorite place. But one day, everything changed. An enemy army attacked Israel. "You're coming with me!" a soldier barked. The young girl never saw her home or family again.

She became a servant. Her job was to take care of a very important woman. So

every day, it was cook, clean, scrub. Then the next day–cook, clean, scrub. And the next, and the next, and the next.

This very important woman whom the girl served was married to a very important man. His name was Naaman. Naaman was a brave soldier for the enemy army that attacked Israel. He was the king's most trusted commander.

But Naaman had a disease.

It made his skin sick with splotches and sores. And everyone could see it. But worst of all, this sickness could kill him.

The young servant girl who worked for Naaman saw his sores, just like everyone else did. And even though he and his fellow soldiers had taken away her freedom, her home, and her family, she was sad that he was sick. Bitterness should have grown up in her heart. But the young girl didn't let it. She let love grow there instead.

"I want the commander to get better," she told Naaman's wife. "And God loves to make people better. There is a man back home who hears from God and speaks for Him. God works miracles through this man.

God will heal Naaman if he goes to him."

So Naaman went. He loaded up riches and fine clothes to pay for his healing and went to see the prophet Elisha, who listened to God and spoke His messages.

Naaman's grand parade pulled up at the prophet Elisha's house. "I'm ready for my healing!" he told the man who had come out to greet him.

"I'm not Elisha. I'm just a messenger," the man said. "Here is what you are supposed to do: Go and wash in the Jordan River seven times, and you won't be sick anymore." Then the messenger went back inside.

"The man of God didn't even come out to see me!" Naaman grumbled. "I thought for sure that he would stand in front of me, talk to his God, and his God would heal me right then. Then I would pay him, and we'd be off! But he wants me to wash in a river? I could have washed in a river at home! This God of his isn't so mighty. Let's go home!" he told his servants.

Naaman was angry. He was insulted. And it was true—God could have healed Naaman on the spot through Elisha, just like Naaman wanted. But God wasn't interested in only healing Naaman's sick body. God also wanted to heal his heart. God wanted Naaman to trust in Him.

"Master," one of Naaman's servants replied, "please do what the messenger said." Another servant added, "You're always so kind to us, and we don't want you to be sick anymore. Wouldn't you do anything to get better—even do something as strange as wash seven times in a foreign river?"

"You're right," Naaman replied. "I *would* do anything to get better.

Let's go to this Jordan River."

So Naaman trusted Elisha's instructions. He dipped once, twice ... seven times in the Jordan River. And as he rose out of the water the seventh time, his skin was perfectly healed! And his heart was healed, too. "This God is real and true!" he declared. "He is the only God! He can do anything! And I will follow Him."

Naaman began to walk with God. And he did so all because a girl who could have grown bitterness in her heart let love grow there instead.

God loves everyone—every single person. And like the servant girl, you can help show other people God's love. Even people who have hurt your heart.

God is good, and you can help other people see how good He is, too. When someone you know is going through something hard, you can ask God to help. If someone you know is sick, you can make them a card and let them know that you are asking God to make them well.

God is good and kind, so when you do good and kind things, you are like an arrow pointing to God. And maybe, like Naaman, the people in your life who don't know God will follow that arrow straight back to Him.

GOD AND HIS ANGEL ARMIES

There is more going on around you
than just what you see.

2 Kings 6:8-23

God's people were still following the evil gods* of their neighbors. It was awful. But even so, God didn't give up on them. He sent prophets to speak His words and perform His miracles–prophets like Elisha. It was God's way of telling His people, "I'm here! I'm good! Even though you've done wrong, I still love you! Come back to Me!"

God's people were at war, but God was telling Elisha every move the enemy king was going to make.

"Go tell the king not to move his army to the valley," Elisha told his messenger. "God told me the enemy king and his army are headed that way."

The servant rushed off to relay the message.

Over and over, God told Elisha what the enemy king and his army were going to do. It was army hide-and-seek. And God was making sure His people's army was always one step ahead of the enemy.

"Who is spying on me?" the enemy king bellowed to his officers.

"No one's spying, sir," one of his officers responded. "But God speaks to a prophet named Elisha and tells him every single thing you say!"

"I must capture this Elisha!" the king roared.

The king sent his strongest army to Dothan–the city where Elisha was. Under the cover of darkness, horses, chariots, and dangerous men snuck into position. As the morning sun rose, the city and the hill it sat atop were surrounded by the mighty army. There was no way out for Elisha.

Elisha's servant woke up early. His jaw dropped when he saw the enemy army.

"Master! Master!" he whispered in a panic, running back to get Elisha. Elisha stepped outside and saw the army. Even though he knew the army was there to capture him, he was not afraid–not one little bit.

"What are we going to do?" his servant asked, terrified.

"Please don't be scared," Elisha answered. "There are so many more fighters on our side than on their side."

What is my master talking about? Elisha's servant wondered. *We're surrounded!*

"Dear God," Elisha prayed, "please help my servant see what is really going on."

All of a sudden, the servant could see. He and Elisha were surrounded alright–by God's angel army. There were chariots upon chariots and even more chariots. And horses upon horses and even more horses, too. And they were all were made of fire! They were commanded by the most powerful riders you can imagine.

God's forces stood strong and mighty, encircled around Elisha and his servant. Their presence said, *If you want to get to God's servant, you have to go through us.*

The enemy army approached Elisha, but he showed no fear. "God, make these men blind," he prayed. And God did. Elisha led the enemy army away from the city. They didn't capture him or cause a single bit of harm.

God tells us in the Bible that there is more going on in the world than just what we can see. Part of what we can't see is that there are angels among us! God has an entire army of angels—thousands upon thousands upon thousands of them. And He has given them great power. Angels are God's good and mighty warriors.

God sends these angels to protect and to help us. So if you need help, ask God for it. You are His friend, and He loves you very much.

And then know this: When you're facing something difficult and you feel all alone, you never are. If you could see what is really going on, you'd see that God is right there with you—and He may have sent His angels, too.

CHAPTER FIFTEEN

THE KING WHO ASKED FOR GOD'S HELP

God loves it when you ask for His help,
and He loves to help you.

2 Kings 18-19

God's people were in big trouble. King Hezekiah's three officials looked out over the walls of Jerusalem down at the huge enemy army below. The Assyrians had attacked nearly all of the cities in the Promised Land and had defeated them.

Jerusalem, the capital, was the only city left. And now the Assyrian army was crouched before it like a tiger, ready to pounce.

The king of Assyria sent one of his officers to deliver a message. He stood outside the city and yelled, so even God's people on the city wall could hear him.

"This is a message from my master, the great king of Assyria!" the messenger bellowed. "We are going to attack this city. We will defeat you. Do not listen to King Hezekiah when he tells you that your God is going to rescue you. He won't. Our armies are too strong. But if you make a peace treaty with us, we will spare you. Otherwise, you're doomed!"

King Hezekiah's officials relayed the message to him. And he became very sad. He knew that God wouldn't want His people to make a peace treaty with the Assyrians because they were so wicked.

King Hezekiah went straight to God's house to talk to Him. And he

sent a message to the prophet Isaiah, who heard from God and spoke for Him. Then the king waited to hear what God had to say.

God told Isaiah His answer. "Tell Hezekiah not to be scared," God said. "I know what the king of Assyria has said about Me. He thinks I am weak. But I am going to make it so he returns back to his country in defeat."

The king of Assyria would not give up. He wrote King Hezekiah a letter. It said: "I hear that God told you I am not going to defeat you. Don't believe Him. My country has attacked many other countries who believed in many different gods. And their gods weren't able to save them. Your God isn't going to save you either."

King Hezekiah took the letter and ran back to God's house. He spread it out before God and talked to Him about it.

"God," King Hezekiah prayed. "You are the King who is in charge of every single king and kingdom. You made all things, and You are over all things. God, the king of Assyria is making fun of You! He is saying You are weak. While it is true that his nation has defeated many other nations and toppled their gods, their gods are false! You are the only God You are *our* God

So please save us from this evil king."

Again, God answered through His prophet Isaiah. "I have heard your prayer, Hezekiah," God said. "And this is what I say to this evil king of Assyria: 'You have dared to speak proudly and arrogantly against Me, the one, true God. You boast about your strength. But I made you. And I am in charge of you. So I am going to put a bit in your mouth like you are a horse, and I am going to lead you back where you came from. You will not harm My people.'

"King Hezekiah," God continued, "I want you to know that the evil king of Assyria will not shoot one single arrow inside of this city. He won't enter Jerusalem because I will guard it Myself. You are My people, and I will take care of you."

That night, God sent one of His angels to the army of Assyria. And that one angel wiped out almost all of the enemy soldiers. The king of Assyria hardly had any army left. He took down his tents and headed back home, never firing a single arrow on God's city.

King Hezekiah had been in serious trouble. And his first response wasn't to solve the problem himself. He could have gathered up his army or sent messages to other nations to help him. But he didn't. He went straight to God. And God answered.

When you have a problem, before you do anything, go to God. Talk to Him about it. Ask Him to help you. He is in charge of all things, so there is no one more important to talk with. He loves it when you come to Him for help, and He loves to help you. And when your difficult problem is over, you'll know that it was God who got you through.

CHAPTER SIXTEEN

WHEN GOD SHOWS HIS POWERFUL GOODNESS

God is holy. | Isaiah 6:1-8

Isaiah loved God very much. He was God's good friend. But most of God's people who lived during Isaiah's time didn't love God and were doing evil things.

One day, God appeared to Isaiah and showed him something very special. God let Isaiah see into heaven—and into His very throne room.

God was seated on His throne, ruling over everything. His long, long robe cascaded down, filling the entire room! Fiery angels flew above Him, announcing His goodness loudly and proudly.

"God is holy, holy, holy. He is good and perfect, and He rules over all. The whole world is filled to the brim with His goodness and love!"

Their voices shook the room.

Isaiah's heart pounded. His knees knocked. His mind flooded with wonder. He was in God's presence! And God was so perfect. So powerful. So good. So loving. So overwhelming! It was more than Isaiah could bear.

"God is so good that I don't deserve to be here!"

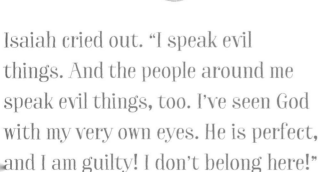

Isaiah cried out. "I speak evil things. And the people around me speak evil things, too. I've seen God with my very own eyes. He is perfect, and I am guilty! I don't belong here!"

One of the fiery angels flew to Isaiah carrying a hot coal from God's altar. The angel reached out until the coal

touched Isaiah's lips. "This has cleaned away the guilt from all of the sinful things you've done," he said. "God has paid for your sins. He has forgiven you."

Right away, Isaiah's shame disappeared. He felt peace. God had paid for his sins! He didn't feel so out of place in God's perfect presence anymore.

Then God Himself spoke from the throne. "I need someone to speak to My people for Me. Who will do it?"

"I'll do it, God!" Isaiah answered. "Send me!" Isaiah spent the rest of his life listening to God and telling the people what God said. And a lot of times, the messages Isaiah shared weren't easy. God's people were turning away from Him, and God was going to have to do something drastic to get their attention— He was going to let His people be taken captive by another nation. So the messages from God that Isaiah delivered weren't always fun. The people didn't like

him very much. But Isaiah followed God, no matter what anyone else said. And Isaiah's love made God very happy.

As Isaiah saw, God is perfection and pure goodness. He is so good and so pure that any speck of evil in our hearts stands out when we're near Him. Each one of us is stained with sin, so none of us can come into God's perfect presence on our own. That's why Isaiah felt ashamed and uncomfortable. He wanted to be close to God, but he couldn't because of his sin. We have the same problem, too.

But God loves us so much! Not being close to us just won't do. So He came up with a solution. He sent His Son Jesus to earth. Jesus never, ever sinned–not one black speck of sin stained His life. He gave His perfect life to pay the cost for every single one of the sins we've committed. Then He beat death and came back to life. And He offers this new life to us.

Jesus says this to you: "I have paid for your sins. And even though you haven't lived a perfect life, I did. I want to give you My perfect, clean, unstained life so that you can come close to Me and live in My love. So let's trade–your sin stains for My spotless life. When you make that trade with Me, you can come close to Me because I have made you as perfect and holy as I am. Not only that, but I can come close to you. I'll never leave you."

Have you talked to God and accepted this trade? God is very excited to make you clean and new so you can come close to Him! He tells us in the Bible that there's a huge party in heaven with the angels each time a person is washed clean from their sins. Hooray!

CHAPTER SEVENTEEN

THE MAN WHO OBEYED GOD ABOVE ALL ELSE

God loves it when you are faithful to Him, no matter what.
Daniel 6

God's people hadn't loved or followed Him for years and years. The time had come to do something drastic to get their attention. Maybe, just maybe, they'd turn their hearts back to Him. So God let His people be attacked. And defeated. And taken captive by an enemy nation–Babylon. God's people were taken away from their comfy, familiar home and brought to a place where everyone spoke a different language and ate strange food, and where no one loved God.

A young man named Daniel was one of the captives taken to Babylon. Since he was smart and handsome, Babylon's leaders sent Daniel to a special school to learn how to speak and live like an excellent Babylonian. They wanted Daniel to become

one of them—to forget that he was a follower of God. But Daniel didn't. While he did his very best in his Babylon studies, he didn't let them pull him away from God.

Daniel lived the rest of his life in this strange land. Every day he honored God by doing his best in everything.

When Daniel was very old, he was given an important position. He was made a leader of leaders. He did such a good job that the king was going to make Daniel his right-hand man—second in command over the entire nation! But when the other leaders heard about it, they got jealous. "We've got to find a way to get that Daniel in trouble!" they schemed.

But they couldn't find anything wrong with Daniel. He was always kind, worked hard, and did his very best. "The only way we can get Daniel in trouble," the other leaders plotted, "is to make it illegal to follow his God."

"Your Majesty, King Darius," they said, appearing before the king. "We have an idea. You are an excellent king. So why don't you make a law that no one can pray to anyone but you for the next 30 days? If anyone breaks this law, they'll be thrown into a den of lions. Isn't this a great idea? Write it down as a new law so it can't be changed."

The king was flattered. "What a wonderful idea. Let's do it! Put the order in writing!"

And so it was. Daniel heard about the law, but it didn't keep him from following God. *I must obey God above any law in this land,* he told himself. So he went up to his room like he did every morning, noon, and night. He opened the windows that looked out in the direction of the Promised Land, his home. He got down on his knees, and he talked to God, his Friend, just like he always did.

"Daniel is praying! I can see him through the window!" one of the leaders sniveled from down below. "Let's get him!"

The men ran back to the king. "King Darius! King Darius!" they cried. "Daniel is praying to God! He's breaking your law and not honoring you!" The king was sad. He liked Daniel and didn't want him to get hurt. But there was nothing he could do—a law was a law. The situation seemed hopeless.

Daniel was brought to the lions' den and thrown in. "Daniel, I know you love your God," the king called after him. "May He rescue you!" A huge stone

was rolled over the den's entrance. Daniel was sealed up with the lions.

That night at the palace, the king couldn't eat. He couldn't sleep. At the first light of dawn, he sprinted to the lions' den and had the stone rolled away.

"Daniel!" he cried. "You serve the living God! Was He able to save you?"

"My God did!" Daniel answered back. "He sent an angel to shut the mouths of the lions! God protected me. I am fine!"

The king was overjoyed. He had Daniel lifted out of the den, safe and sound. He ordered the evil men who trapped Daniel to be thrown in with the lions. Then the king issued a decree: "Daniel's God is the one, true God. He rules over all. Everyone in my kingdom must honor Daniel's God."

Sometimes, the laws of our land will go against God's ways. But God's children are citizens of God's kingdom, first and foremost. When it costs us to follow God and His ways, God sees and knows. He is honored by our faithfulness, and He will take care of us. And sometimes, when we stand up for God's good ways, people around us will see His good heart in what we do.

CHAPTER EIGHTEEN

GOD'S GREAT CONSTRUCTION PROJECT

God loves it when you're faithful with everyday things.
Nehemiah 1–6

To draw *His people back to Him,* God allowed them to be taken captive to a faraway land. But He promised it would only be for a little while–and God always keeps His promises. So after about 70 years, God made it so His people could return home. Some of them did. But back home, God's people discovered something terrible. The Promised Land was a mess. Cities were rubble heaps. Homes were trash piles. God's house was a burned ruin. Their home was a disaster area. So the people started rebuilding–stone by stone, brick by brick. But the wall around the city of Jerusalem remained a broken-down pile of rubble.

Nehemiah was one of God's people who had

chosen to stay in the foreign land. He had an important job—cupbearer to the king. (He would taste the king's drink to make sure there wasn't any poison in it.) But even though he had stayed in Persia, Nehemiah loved God and God's land.

When Nehemiah's brother, Hanani, came to visit, Nehemiah asked how the people were doing back in the Promised Land.

Hanani's news wasn't good. "The people who have gone back home are very sad," he said. "The capital city's walls are in shambles."

In those days, a city's walls were very important. Without them, a city would be an easy target for enemies. Tall, strong walls stood like a bodyguard, showing everyone that the city was powerful.

Nehemiah cried and cried. These were God's people, and this was God's land! They should be proud of their city, not ashamed!

So Nehemiah talked to God, His friend. "God, we are Your people. You promised that if we turned away from our sin and turned back to You, You would bring us back home. But Jerusalem, our city—Your city—is a mess. We need Your help. When I go to the king, please let him give me permission to go back home and rebuild the walls."

God heard and answered His friend. He made it so that the king of Persia allowed Nehemiah to leave. The King even gave Nehemiah all the building materials he would need! God took care of everything.

When Nehemiah got to Jerusalem, he rode a donkey around the city at night, inspecting the walls. The next day, he gathered God's people together. "The walls are in shambles," he told them. "Let's rebuild them so we won't be ashamed anymore. I'm here to help!"

"Let's do it!" the people chimed in. And they got to work.

Chisel, chisel, chisel. Pound, pound, pound. The city became one big construction site. Everyone came out to build the walls. Up, up, and up they went.

But the neighbors around Jerusalem didn't like it. They didn't want Jerusalem to be a strong city. So they made fun of God's people. "You're doing a terrible job!" they taunted. "That wall is so puny that just a fox walking on top of it would knock it down!"

Their insults got even worse: "We're going to attack you so you can't build anymore!" God's people got scared.

"Don't be afraid!" Nehemiah encouraged. "God is with you, and those enemies are no match for Him! Keep building!" So some of God's people held weapons in one hand and building tools in the other. But they kept working and working. Up, up, and up went the walls.

Since their first attempts to stop the building project weren't successful, the enemies of God's people tried to scare Nehemiah by luring him outside the city to hurt him. But Nehemiah didn't fall for it. "I'm doing a great work, and I can't stop," he told them.

Up, up, and up went the walls. Every day, despite the obstacles, the people worked faithfully. And soon, they were finished! The city was surrounded and guarded by strong, tall, powerful walls. The people were proud. Nehemiah was proud. And God was proud, too.

God loves it when you're faithful. He loves it when you do what you're supposed to do every day—no matter what distractions there are, no matter what other people say. Following God with every single choice, with every single step, may not seem like a big deal. But you'll find, as Nehemiah did, that God uses every small step and every single choice to build a great work in you.

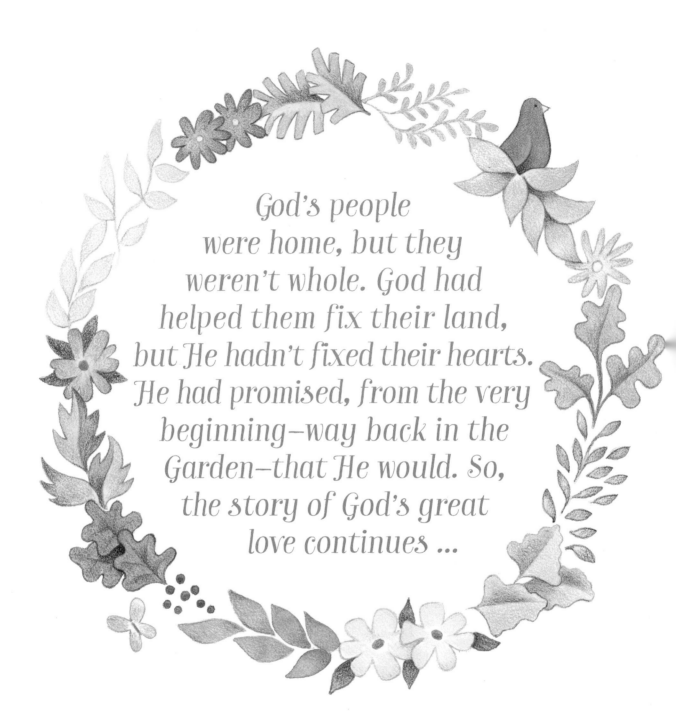

God's people
were home, but they
weren't whole. God had
helped them fix their land,
but He hadn't fixed their hearts.
He had promised, from the very
beginning—way back in the
Garden—that He would. So,
the story of God's great
love continues ...

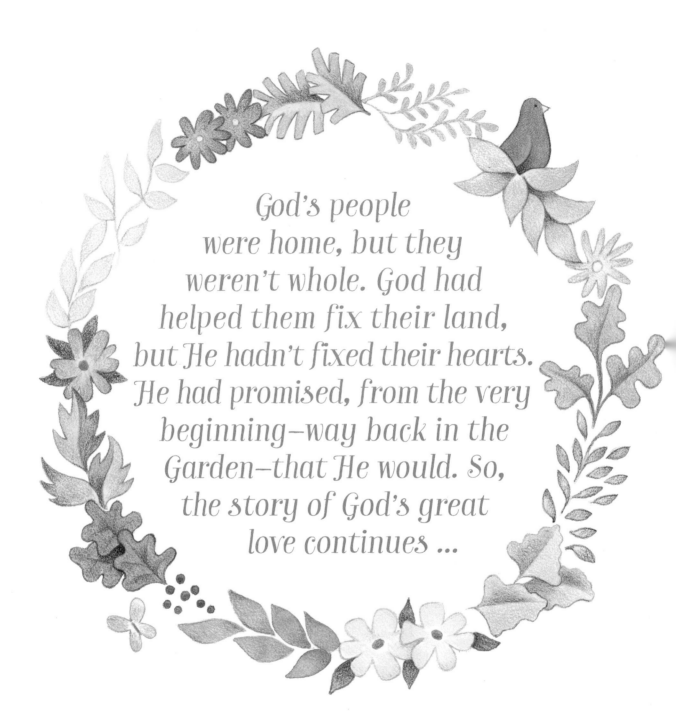

A WORD FROM THE AUTHOR

LAURIN GRECO: As a mother, I feel there are two foundational truths that I strive to plant deep within my child's heart: *God is good,* and *He loves you very much.* So in each of these Old Testament stories, I put a spotlight on God's heart to help kids see the goodness that's already there.

I wrote this Bible storybook for parents like me, and for grandparents–so we can take hold of every opportunity we have to train up a generation rooted in God's goodness and in His great love.

A WORD FROM THE ILLUSTRATOR

JEFF GREGORY: It was important to me that the illustrations accurately reflect the biblical stories–as much as possible for a children's book. These stories may be a child's first exposure to God's Word, and the images they see can shape their understanding of Scripture for years to come. As a child's guide into the world of the Bible, my hope is to show them God's power and goodness through these drawings.